THE SCARLET LETTER

By

PHYLLIS NAGY

ADAPTED FROM THE NOVEL BY
Nathaniel Hawthorne

S A M U E L F R E N C H , I N C.
45 WEST 25TH STREET   NEW YORK 10010
7623 SUNSET BOULEVARD   HOLLYWOOD 90046
LONDON   *TORONTO*

IMPORTANT BILLING AND CREDIT REQUIREMENTS

THE SCARLET LETTER was commissioned and produced by the Denver Center Theatre Company, Donovan Marley, Artistic Director. The first production opened March 21, 1994 with the following cast:

HESTER PRYNNE............................. Jacqueline Antaramian
MASTER BRACKETT............................. Michael Hartman
PEARL.. Sara Fernandez-K
MISTRESS HIBBINS............................. Suzanne Bouchard
GOVERNOR BELLINGHAM........................ Michael Santo
ARTHUR DIMMESDALE............................ Sean Hennigan
ROGER CHILLINGWORTH........................... Richard Risso

Directed by - Jamie Horton
Sets and Costumes by - Andrew V. Yelusich
Lighting by - Don Darnutzer

It subsequently opened in New York on October 11, 1994 in a production by the Classic Stage Company, David Esbjornson, Artistic Director with the following cast:

HESTER PRYNNE... Cynthia Nixon
MASTER BRACKETT.. Dan Daily
PEARL.. Erin Cressida Wilson
MISTRESS HIBBINS.. Sheila Tousey
GOVERNOR BELLINGHAM...................... Bill Cwikowski
ARTHUR DIMMESDALE........................... Stephen Caffrey
ROGER CHILLINGWORTH............................. Jon De Vries

Directed by - Lisa Peterson

THE CHARACTERS

Hester Prynne: A Stunning young seamstress who's a master of irony. She is neither sentimental nor self-pitying. Her defiant humor sees her through most situations. Late 20's.

Arthur Dimmesdale: A successful young minister who finds it difficult to trust anybody. Sexy and rather capable, though he doesn't think so. Late 20's.

Roger Chillingworth: A 50-something, humpbacked, would-be physician who's slipped into an early old age. Possessed of a dry and deadly wit.

Pearl: Hester's daughter, the most unusual child in the world. She must be played by an actress in her late 20's, who at no time attempts to play her as a child.

Governor Bellingham: Boston's Governor. Well-meaning but pompous.

Master Brackett: Boston's jailer. Kind, and the slightest bit slow on the uptake.

Mistress Hibbins: Boston's witch, and sister to Governor Bellingham. Just past 30, and maddeningly sexy.

TIME, PLACE AND SETTING

The events of The Scarlet Letter take place some 300 years ago, in Boston, Mass.

There are several set pieces which, at first glance, seem to bear no naturalistic relationship to each other, but which instead might appear to float together in the same space; an enormous prison doorway, the portal of which is surrounded by a wild rose bush; a balcony overlooking that doorway; a graveyard; and a large scaffold. Beyond these things and closing in on them is a vast expanse of wood--suffocating, threatening, infinite and completely dominating the environment.

It is always summer.

PLAYWRIGHT'S NOTE:

The scarlet letter itself should be a dazzling bit of costume. The scarlet letter is Hester's one luxurious accessory, and she wears it well. While she clothes herself quite austerely, she makes incredibly beautiful, indeed decadent, clothing for her daughter.

ACT I

(Lights up on the prison doorway. From the surrounding darkness, HESTER speaks.)

HESTER. I made it myself. There was no other way. I searched every shop in Boston to no avail. The scarlet letter could not be bought. So I started from scratch.

(Lights up on HESTER PRYNNE and BRACKETT behind the doorway. HESTER wears a simple dress and bonnet. Brackett tries to help HESTER fasten the scarlet letter to her bosom.)

HESTER. It took me quite some time to find the gold silk thread. Gold is precious and so I had to have it for my letter. If I am to keep nothing but the scarlet letter, it must be special.

(BRACKETT pricks himself.)

BRACKETT. Ouch. Christ. Sorry.

HESTER. You mustn't be so careful with it, Master Brackett. Let me show you. *(HESTER takes BRACKETT'S hand and guides it high up on her bosom.)* Fasten it here. I adore pretty things. Master Brackett?

BRACKETT. Mistress Prynne.

HESTER. Why do you hesitate?

BRACKETT. Isn't this improper?
HESTER. At the very least.

(BRACKETT drops the scarlet letter. HESTER laughs and begins to fasten the letter herself.)

HESTER. Do you know how costly gold silk thread is, Master Brackett?
BRACKETT. *(Shrugs.)* I'm a jailer.
HESTER. Take a guess. Humor me.
BRACKETT. I'm humorless.

(HESTER finishes fastening the scarlet letter.)

HESTER. I despise self-pity, Master Brackett.

(A bell strikes noon.)

BRACKETT. I mean you no harm, Mistress Prynne.
HESTER I asked you to help me affix my punishment. There is nothing improper in that.
BRACKETT. We should go.

(BRACKETT holds out his arm to HESTER. She doesn't take it.)

HESTER. Bring me my child.

(Lights up on PEARL. She seems to come forward, as she speaks, from the vast expanse of wood, right down to the edge of the scaffold.)

PEARL. My first three months are spent in that prison. Unlike my mother, I have no affection for pretty things. Nor do I care for our jailer, Master Brackett, who shudders every time he edges past my cradle. A nice man, though. But I don't like nice men. I like the woods.

(The bell continues to toll. HESTER and BRACKETT listen to it for several beats, then:)

HESTER. Are you married, Master Brackett?

BRACKETT. Thirty years.

HESTER. What is your wife's name?

BRACKETT. Charlotte. We met in Bristol. I was a milkman. She baked bread.

HESTER. And here we are in Boston. *(A beat.)* I lived in Amsterdam.

BRACKETT. I've always meant to see the canals.

HESTER. Yes. Well. You've missed nothing.

PEARL. I like the woods. Like the feel of the trees swaying dangerously above me, the threat of a sudden disaster. Hester courts punishment, but me, I crave catastrophe, the slightest hint of it. And today's my first treat.

BRACKETT. It's noon. Past noon.

HESTER. I know.

BRACKETT. Mistress Prynne, I am sorry.

HESTER. Is it nice in Bristol?

BRACKETT. I don't remember.

HESTER. You're sweating, Master Brackett. Your upper lip is very wet. *(Beat.)* Bring me my Pearl.

BRACKETT. They say if you expose an infant to crowds, it will grow to fear human contact.

HESTER. I'll take my chances.

PEARL. I love a woman who gambles even more than I love the woods. Master Brackett passes me to Hester as if I'm an infectious disease. And so I meet Boston.

(HESTER and BRACKETT cross the prison doorway's threshold. At no time should HESTER pretend to have a child in her arms, nor should BRACKETT mime bringing her a child. HESTER holds her hands over her chest, as if to hide the scarlet letter from view. PEARL reaches the edge of the scaffold. Lights up on the balcony to reveal GOVERNOR BELLINGHAM, ARTHUR DIMMESDALE and MISTRESS HIBBINS, who smiles and waves to an unseen crowd as if she is a very great dignitary.)

BELLINGHAM. Hester Prynne: Who is the child's father? Your silence is inexplicable.

HESTER. I will not name him.

BELLINGHAM: Hester Prynne: Look about you. The whole of Boston awaits your response. Do not disappoint us.

HESTER. I will not name him.

PEARL. It's a fine summer's day in the marketplace and the swell of people pressed close, so close to our scaffold, eager for humiliation, excites me. I look directly at the sun, having never before seen it. My eyes burn. I pinch Hester's breast.

(HESTER shudders, as if in response to the pinch.)

HIBBINS. *(To Bellingham.)* Look, brother. It's Cooper, the silversmith. And over there, that miserly butcher, Wright. I never thought I'd see the day he closed shop for a—

BELLINGHAM. Be still, sister. Have you no sense of propriety?

HIBBINS. I love a good public scolding. *(To HESTER.)* Adulteress!

HESTER. Witch.

(BELLINGHAM, BRACKETT and HIBBINS are momentarily taken aback. DIMMESDALE is quite still.)

BELLINGHAM. Left to my own devices, Hester Prynne, I would lock you away from our citizenry for the rest of your days. Fortunately for you, our good Reverend Dimmesdale prevails upon me to exercise mercy.

HESTER. Is there a man among you who is sinless, Governor?

(MISTRESS HIBBINS laughs.)

BELLINGHAM. Your arrogance compounds your sin. You will be silent, Mistress Prynne! Silent!

HESTER. I have no wish other than to be silent, Governor. But I will not name the child's father.

(Thunder is heard in the distance. HESTER and PEARL begin to ascend the scaffold. DIMMESDALE steps forward and calls out to HESTER.)

DIMMESDALE. Hester!

(Thunder. It's much closer. HESTER turns towards DIMMESDALE. They regard each other calmly.)

PEARL. He calls out to her: Hester. Hester. My mother is mesmerized by no man, and yet, she is mesmerized by this man. I take immediately against him. Hester removes me from her breast and reveals our letter to the crowd. The hush is enormous.

(HESTER and PEARL resume their ascent to the scaffold. Lightning, as HESTER reaches the top of the scaffold and slowly removes her hands from her chest to reveal the scarlet letter to BELLINGHAM and DIMMESDALE.)

BELLINGHAM. What is she doing? What does that woman think she's *doing.*

DIMMESDALE. She is taking her place among us, Governor.

(Thunder. It's very near. ROGER CHILLINGWORTH appears beside BRACKETT, as if from nowhere. CHILLINGWORTH carries a small black bag. HIBBINS' attention is focused on CHILLINGWORTH.)

BELLINGHAM. She makes a nonsense of her penance.

DIMMESDALE. That letter is extraordinary.

CHILLINGWORTH. *(To BRACKETT.)* What a striking woman.

BRACKETT. A seamstress.

CHILLINGWORTH. What is her name?

HIBBINS. *(Calling out to CHILLINGWORTH.)* Adulteress!

CHILLINGWORTH. A woman as striking as she is worthy of adultery.

(More thunder, as if punctuation to CHILLINGWORTH'S comment.)

HIBBINS. *(Calling out to HESTER.)* Who's the father? We want the child's father. We want his blood.

BELLINGHAM. The citizenry demands your response, Mistress Prynne.

HESTER. Never.

(Thunder, lightning. It's terrifying.)

PEARL. The trees rock violently, Hester shivers and I am happy. Such a happy baby. The storm approaches.

DIMMESDALE. Hester. There is a way to spare yourself a lonely indignity. Is it not proper to share the burden of punishment?

HESTER. I prefer my own company.

BRACKETT. *(To CHILLINGWORTH.)* Why don't I know you?

CHILLINGWORTH. I've come from the woods. I'm a doctor.

BRACKETT. I don't know many doctors who come from the woods.

CHILLINGWORTH. Your minister is ill.

DIMMESDALE. Hester, will you not give us his name? A better fate awaits him should you name him.

HESTER. How?

DIMMESDALE. I... pardon?

HESTER. A better fate. How does it await him?

DIMMESDALE. Well, we presume. We trust... that it does.

HESTER. I don't.

(PEARL raises her hand and points to DIMMESDALE. DIMMESDALE falls to his knees. He places his hand over his heart. Thunder, lightning. It's a violent storm.)

CHILLINGWORTH. I told you. Your minister is ill. See how he falls.

BRACKETT. But you come from the woods. How did you know?

BELLINGHAM. Hester Prynne: Your indifference grieves our good minister.

HESTER. I am anything but indifferent.

DIMMESDALE. *(To BELLINGHAM.)* Leave her. It's no use. She won't speak.

PEARL. The minister speaks. I scream.

BELLINGHAM. *(To HESTER.)* Calm that child.

(HESTER remains still.)

HIBBINS. *(To CHILLINGWORTH.)* The infant speaks to us.

CHILLINGWORTH. Indeed.

HESTER. The child will not be calmed, Governor, as the storm will not be calmed.

BELLINGHAM. Hester Prynne: Sentence cannot be delayed. You--and you child who will not be calmed--will remain on the scaffold this day for a period of three hours. And you will be looked upon by every citizen of Boston and you will wear the letter of the adulteress upon your person for the rest of your days, Hester Prynne.

PEARL. And then it happens. A mighty storm descends, the crowd disperses in fear, and a chill seizes Hester as surely as a noose might tighten about her neck.

(CHILLINGWORTH takes a step towards the scaffold. DIMMESDALE watches him.)

CHILLINGWORTH. Hester Prynne: Give us his name. The child's father. Tell us his name.

(A great crack of thunder as HESTER and CHILLINGWORTH regard each other.)

HESTER. I have said all that I mean to say, sir.

(CHILLINGWORTH moves towards HESTER.)

DIMMESDALE. I don't feel at all well.
BELLINGHAM. Heartbreak.
DIMMESDALE. Surely it's just a simple stomach upset. There's no need—
BELLINGHAM. Heartbreak and disappointment. A young member of your flock gone astray.

(More lightning, thunder. CHILLINGWORTH stands at the edge of the scaffold and holds out his hand as if to calm PEARL.)

PEARL. And I who will not be calmed am calmed by this humpbacked old man with a black bag. He's extraordinarily ugly. But I adore him.
CHILLINGWORTH. Will you not tell me his name, Hester Prynne?

(Lights down on all but CHILLINGWORTH and HESTER. A Silence. CHILLINGWORTH holds out his hand to HESTER and helps her down from the scaffold. He opens his bag and from it removes a small vial of liquid, which he sets down between himself and HESTER. He examines HESTER thoroughly: eyes, ears, mouth, throat, reflexes--the works. They speak throughout the examination.)

CHILLINGWORTH. The child is fine. No fever. A healthy set of lungs.

HESTER. Her name is Pearl.

CHILLINGWORTH. Of course, she may yet prove to be ill. Such bad weather lately. So cold.

HESTER. My daughter is called Pearl.

CHILLINGWORTH. And so unpredictable. The storm this afternoon, for instance. A freak cloudburst, one might say. Which began precisely at the moment you stepped upon the scaffold and ended precisely at the moment you stepped back inside this prison. The coincidence of weather is thrilling. Don't you think? *(A beat.)* The child is quiet now. She took to the draught.

HESTER. You're remarkably unattractive. *(A beat.)* And your hump. It's grown.

(HESTER reaches out to touch CHILLINGWORTH'S hump. He grabs her hand.)

CHILLINGWORTH. Do not touch me.

HESTER. I admire deformity.

(CHILLINGWORTH offers the vial of liquid to HESTER.)

CHILLINGWORTH. Cruelty becomes you.

HESTER. Will you poison me? You've already poisoned my child.

CHILLINGWORTH. If that's true, you stood by and watched it happen. *(Beat.)* You look old, Hester. Punished.

HESTER. Let me touch your hump.

CHILLINGWORTH. Take the draught.

HESTER. You make an odd doctor. And what do you call yourself now?

CHILLINGWORTH. Roger Chillingworth. Take the draught, Hester.

(HESTER does. She then reaches out to touch Chillingworth's hump. He again stops her. He traces the outline of the scarlet letter with one finger.)

CHILLINGWORTH. You're good with a needle.

HESTER. I took your medicine, Mister Chillingworth. Now leave me.

CHILLINGWORTH. Stunning work. And the child, she's a stunning piece of work as well.

HESTER. *(After a beat.)* I never loved you.

CHILLINGWORTH. My argument is not with you, Hester.

(CHILLINGWORTH places HESTER'S hand on his hump.)

HESTER. I don't remember you being so ugly.

CHILLINGWORTH. I was ugly when I married you.

HESTER. You sent no word. I waited two years. I could wait no longer.

CHILLINGWORTH. I was gaining knowledge. Touch me.

(CHILLINGWORTH moves HESTER'S hand along his back.)

CHILLINGWORTH. It was with reluctance I left the woods, Hester. But I do not question my hunches and I had this hunch about you. An urge to track you down again. Boston will know me as a physician, Hester. A healer. Do not lead people to believe otherwise.

HESTER. You had a kindness about you once. A gratefulness. When I brought you tea or woke you from a nightmare you looked at me with such decency.

(CHILLINGWORTH removes HESTER'S hand from his back.)

CHILLINGWORTH. The draught has not killed you. See?

HESTER. You won't be staying long in Boston. If you don't plan to claim me as your wife.

CHILLINGWORTH. The town needs a good doctor. I'll stay.

HESTER. You're not a doctor.

CHILLINGWORTH. I can isolate a sickness. Cure an ailment. Administer to grief. I've used these two years wisely, Hester. Have you?

HESTER. I have Pearl.

CHILLINGWORTH. And I will have my vengeance.

HESTER. You have it now.

CHILLINGWORTH. I believe the child's father was present today. In the marketplace. Somewhere in the crowd he was sweating under his collar. And what a crowd there was. You're famous, Hester. All of New England knows your name. And I, a humble doctor, among your admirers. I'll find him, Hester.

HESTER. You've found me. It's enough.

CHILLINGWORTH. I sent you here, it's true. I have myself to blame. But I did not abandon you.

HESTER. No. I abandoned you. Let me abandon you.

(Lights up on PEARL in the graveyard. She picks flowers off the graves.)

CHILLINGWORTH. I will stay in Boston, Hester. And so will you.

HESTER. I might not. I might go elsewhere.

CHILLINGWORTH. You flaunt your sin, Hester. And your punishment. Your vanity will not allow you to leave.

HESTER. We used to sleep together. I fed you when you were ill. I bathed you.

CHILLINGWORTH. I am not a child, Hester. I'm ugly. And my ugliness will find him out. And when I find him, I shall make his torment my life's work.

HESTER. Your life can't last much longer.

CHILLINGWORTH. No. But his can.

HESTER. If I close my eyes, I might convince myself you're handsome. You could be Pearl's father.

CHILLINGWORTH. I'm not very paternal, Hester. *(A beat.)* Take care. You will not reveal me to anyone. We will not meet again.

HESTER. I hate you. But I won't betray you.

CHILLINGWORTH. You've already betrayed me. Now keep me a secret.

HESTER. Sometimes I think I'll take Pearl far from here. I'll teach her to read and she'll grow to have many friends. I'll remarry into great wealth. My daughter's popularity will be legendary. *(Beat.)* It's a thought.

CHILLINGWORTH. Beyond here is the woods, Hester. A vast space full of nothing but a threat of the unseen.

HESTER. I said it was only a thought.

CHILLINGWORTH. I know you never loved me. *(Beat.)* I'm certain the child's father is a man of high standing, Hester. Your taste was always impeccable. *(Beat.)* Pearl. What a ridiculous name.

(CHILLINGWORTH exits. HESTER removes her bonnet and shakes loose her hair. She runs her fingers through her hair, as if to comb it out.)

PEARL. Time passes. As it will. We live in a cottage on the outskirts of town, Hester and me. We live in a cottage by the edge of the sea and mostly I speak to no one and no one speaks to me.

(MISTRESS HIBBINS enters the graveyard. She carries a small hand mirror behind her back. Lights fade from HESTER.)

HIBBINS. Oh my. Playing with the dead. What an inventive little girl.

PEARL. Go away.

HIBBINS. And so polite. Your mother's taught you well.

PEARL. You don't know Hester.

HIBBINS. But I do. She's my sister. I'm your aunt.

PEARL. Hester has no friends and I'm her only relative.

HIBBINS. A little girl as bright as you should know of metaphor. Let me tell you about metaphor, Pearl.

(HIBBINS holds out the mirror to PEARL. PEARL looks into the mirror.)

HIBBINS. Tell me, Pearl, what do you see?
PEARL. Dirt.
HIBBINS. And what else?
PEARL. Nothing. Dirt. I have dirt on my face.

(HIBBINS replaces the mirror behind her back.)

HIBBINS. What a vain little girl. You can't stop looking at your own reflection in the glass.
PEARL. They say you're a witch.
HIBBINS. Who says I'm a witch?
PEARL. Everybody.
HIBBINS. But you haven't any friends. Nobody talks to you.
PEARL. Hester doesn't have friends. I have friends, though. Many friends.
HIBBINS. Where are these friends?
PEARL. Here. And there.
HIBBINS. We can be friends. Good friends.
PEARL. You're too old to be my friend.
HIBBINS. I can take you with me to the woods.
PEARL. When?
HIBBINS. At night.
PEARL. And who will we meet?
HIBBINS. My friends. Your mother's friends. The man.
PEARL. Which man?
HIBBINS. The dark man. He owns the woods.
PEARL. Why didn't Hester tell me she had a sister?
HIBBINS. Why do you call your mother by her Christian name?
PEARL. I'm wild. Hester says so.

HIBBINS. Why does your mother wear the scarlet letter?

PEARL. Because it's red. And red is gorgeous.

HIBBINS. No. Guess again.

PEARL. Because it's wild. Like me.

HIBBINS. You are a smart girl. And who gave your mother her pretty letter?

PEARL. Nobody. It's just there.

HIBBINS. I'll tell you a secret. I have a letter, too. So do you. But you can't see them.

PEARL. You're lying. Hester's letter is special.

HIBBINS. It may be special, Pearl, but she got it from somebody. Who gave it to her?

PEARL. The wind. It came from the wind.

HIBBINS. It came from the dark man. And who is the dark man?

PEARL. He lives in the woods.

HIBBINS. That's right. And he's your father, Pearl.

PEARL. I have no father.

HIBBINS. Let me take you to him.

PEARL. When?

HIBBINS. At night.

PEARL. When.

HIBBINS. Soon.

PEARL. How soon?

HIBBINS. Soon enough. *(She holds up the mirror to her own face.)* Look Pearl: What do you see?

(PEARL looks into the mirror with HIBBINS.)

PEARL. I see me.

HIBBINS. And me. You see me. We are the same. We are

from the same place, Pearl. Let's be friends.

PEARL. What will you give me?

HIBBINS. Knowledge, Pearl. I will give you knowledge.

PEARL. Pick flowers with me.

HIBBINS. They're not your flowers.

PEARL. Everything's mine.

HIBBINS. How old are you, Pearl?

PEARL. Seven. I'm lucky. Pick flowers with me. I take them to Hester.

HIBBINS. They're flowers for the dead, Pearl. Not the living. Do you know the difference? Let me teach you the difference.

PEARL. You're dead. Witches are dead.

HIBBINS. If I pick flowers with you, you'll have to come to the woods with me.

PEARL. I like the woods.

HIBBINS. And you'll be my special friend.

PEARL. You laughed at me.

HIBBINS. When? When did I laugh at you?

PEARL. Then. When I stood with Hester. On the scaffold.

HIBBINS. You were an infant when you stood on the scaffold with your mother.

PEARL. I remember.

HIBBINS. I know.

(Lights up on DIMMESDALE and CHILLINGWORTH at the edge of the wood. CHILLINGWORTH appears to be older and more unattractive. DIMMESDALE walks with difficulty and uses a cane. CHILLINGWORTH supports him. They walk toward the graveyard.)

PEARL. Why do you carry a looking glass?

HIBBINS. So I never miss a trick. Why are you such an odd child?

PEARL. I'm not a child. I'm a treasure.

HIBBINS. So you are.

(HIBBINS picks a bit of weed from a grave and holds it out to PEARL.)

PEARL. What's that?

HIBBINS. A gift. From your father.

(PEARL reaches out cautiously for the weed.)

HIBBINS. Take it.

(PEARL suddenly grabs HIBBINS' hand and bites it.)

HIBBINS. *(Nonchalant, as she considers her wound.)* Do you always bite your friends?

PEARL. I'm odd. You said so. Do witches bleed?

(CHILLINGWORTH and DIMMESDALE approach the grave-yard. CHILLINGWORTH carries his black bag.)

HIBBINS. Ask your mother. Ask the minister.

PEARL. *(To DIMMESDALE):* Do witches bleed?

(CHILLINGWORTH laughs. DIMMESDALE is silent.)

CHILLINGWORTH. Good day, Mistress Hibbins. I see

you are busy schooling our young.

HIBBINS. Mister Chillingworth. My favorite physician.

PEARL. Minister. Do witches bleed?

DIMMESDALE. *(He's tentative.)* You should hold your tongue, child. *(A beat.)* Impertinence is dangerous.

PEARL. Is it?

CHILLINGWORTH. Isn't this the Prynne girl?

HIBBINS. The same. A real beauty. Just like her father.

PEARL. I want to know. She said you'd know.

DIMMESDALE. I'm afraid Mistress Hibbins is having a joke at your expense. Shouldn't you be at home?

PEARL. Why? Why should I be at home?

DIMMESDALE. Your mother needs you. *(A beat.)* Surely.

PEARL. I'm playing.

DIMMESDALE. In a graveyard?

PEARL. You live above the graveyard, minister. Is there something wrong with it?

DIMMESDALE. No child. There's nothing wrong with the graveyard.

PEARL. Are you ill?

DIMMESDALE. I've been better.

PEARL. You're always ill. Why are you ill?

DIMMESDALE. Only God knows.

PEARL. I know why.

DIMMESDALE. I'm sure you don't.

PEARL. You're odd. You walk with a cane.

CHILLINGWORTH. Perceptive for her age.

HIBBINS. Like her father.

DIMMESDALE. Mistress Hibbins, that is quite enough. The child is fatherless.

PEARL. Jesus was fatherless.

DIMMESDALE. Who told you that?

PEARL. Hester told me that. You look unwell, minister. Are you unwell?

DIMMESDALE. It is none of your concern.

PEARL. I'm concerned about witches. You should tell me if they bleed.

DIMMESDALE. You need not fear witches, child.

PEARL. I'm not afraid. But you are.

CHILLINGWORTH. Such big thoughts for such a small girl. Go home now, child. You have not business here.

PEARL. *(To DIMMESDALE.)* Will you die soon?

(HESTER enters.)

HESTER. Pearl. Come here.

PEARL. Hester.

(PEARL goes to HESTER.)

HESTER. I turned around and you'd disappeared. Don't ever disappear on me.

PEARL. He scared me.

HESTER. Who scared you?

PEARL. The minister. I was playing and he scared me.

DIMMESDALE. Mistress Prynne, I assure you—

HIBBINS. Good day, Mistress Prynne. Will I see you tonight? Will you ride with me?

(A silence. HESTER takes PEARL'S hand and they exit.)

HIBBINS. Such rudeness. I only asked her a question.

CHILLINGWORTH. Indeed.

HIBBINS. And you, minister. Will you ride with us this evening?

DIMMESDALE. You're bleeding, Mistress Hibbins.

HIBBINS. *(She looks at her bleeding hand):* So it's true after all.

DIMMESDALE. You speak in riddles.

HIBBINS. Do I? *(She laughs.)* We'll meet again, minister.

(HIBBINS exits.)

CHILLINGWORTH. An altogether stimulating woman, don't you think?

DIMMESDALE. Perhaps from a... medical... standpoint.

CHILLINGWORTH. Not at all. She speaks her mind. An attractive quality.

DIMMESDALE. I've never given her a second thought.

CHILLINGWORTH. Why not?

DIMMESDALE. Why should I?

CHILLINGWORTH. Because you're a man.

DIMMESDALE. I'm a busy man.

CHILLINGWORTH. A young man. A potentially vital man.

DIMMESDALE. She's a widow.

CHILLINGWORTH. Precisely. Besides, she's our Governor's sister. A very respectable catch. And she's experienced.

DIMMESDALE. I'd like to rest now. If I may.

CHILLINGWORTH. Surely you've at least an interest in rehabilitating Mistress Hibbins.

DIMMESDALE. She has no desire to be rehabilitated.

CHILLINGWORTH. Clever woman. I am an old man, Arthur.

I've lost my vigor. But if I were still young I would take to Hibbins. I would—

DIMMESDALE. Will you come this Sunday morning to hear my sermon?

CHILLINGWORTH. Will you accompany me to the brothel this Sunday evening? *(A silence. CHILLINGWORTH laughs.)* Arthur. A sense of humor has always eluded you.

DIMMESDALE. I'm not joking.

CHILLINGWORTH. Neither am I.

DIMMESDALE. Seven years. And I'm still eager for you to take an interest in my work.

CHILLINGWORTH. Yes. Rather like a schoolboy.

DIMMESDALE. My schooling's long finished, Roger.

CHILLINGWORTH. We learn something new every day.

DIMMESDALE. What have you learned today?

CHILLINGWORTH. That Mistress Hibbins is remarkably buxom.

DIMMESDALE. I hadn't noticed.

CHILLINGWORTH. You should have. *(Beat.)* Cheer up, Arthur. I take an interest in your health. Why must I also take an interest in your preaching?

DIMMESDALE. Because it is my health.

CHILLINGWORTH. Is it? I've heard differently. I've heard that lately, your sermons are quite inspired. And your illness has become much worse.

DIMMESDALE. Don't believe everything you hear.

CHILLINGWORTH. But I do. People leave the church in tears, Arthur. They are... transported. And you, so ill. One would think you've a vested interest in remaining ill.

DIMMESDALE. I feel better now. Stronger.

CHILLINGWORTH. You're a mess, Arthur. You're shriveling up. You ought to rest.

DIMMESDALE. There is no place to rest here.

CHILLINGWORTH. What better place to rest, Arthur, than in a graveyard? Sit.

(DIMMESDALE sits in the dirt.)

DIMMESDALE. Why do your medicines have no effect on me?

CHILLINGWORTH. Perhaps they do have an effect. *(Beat.)* It's quite a sight. A minister sitting in the dirt of a graveyard.

DIMMESDALE. It's hallowed ground.

CHILLINGWORTH. How do you know?

DIMMESDALE. It's... of course it's hallowed.

CHILLINGWORTH. But how do you know that?

DIMMESDALE. I just do.

CHILLINGWORTH. You question very little, Arthur.

DIMMESDALE. That's the nature of faith.

CHILLINGWORTH. But it's not the nature of living.

DIMMESDALE. The nature of life is inexplicable.

CHILLINGWORTH. Science explains life. And the nature of science is inquisitive.

DIMMESDALE. Curiosity killed the cat, Roger.

CHILLINGWORTH. How do you know?

DIMMESDALE. I... what a preposterous question. It simply... did.

CHILLINGWORTH. Have you ever actually seen curiosity kill a cat?

DIMMESDALE. No, I... it's... difficult to... for goodness sake. It's metaphorical. Very well. If you insist, your logic defeats me.

CHILLINGWORTH. Metaphor is intangible, Arthur. Logic is not. Logic leads to truth. And what is truth?

DIMMESDALE. Do not confuse me. I'm weak. Tired.

CHILLINGWORTH. But you told me you're feeling better. Stronger. The truth is, you're sitting in a pile of dirt.

DIMMESDALE. (*After a considered beat):* I admire you so much, Roger.

CHILLINGWORTH. Mistress Hibbins is quite voluptuous.

DIMMESDALE. She may have murdered her husband.

CHILLINGWORTH. Voluptuous women often do.

DIMMESDALE. Do they?

CHILLINGWORTH. The demands they make. Brutal.

DIMMESDALE. I'm exhausted, Roger.

CHILLINGWORTH. You appeal to me out here, in the open air. Sit awhile. Talk.

DIMMESDALE. I'm not a handsome man.

CHILLINGWORTH. I had a voluptuous wife, once. A buxom wife.

DIMMESDALE. I lack a certain... rugged... quality that appeals to women.

CHILLINGWORTH. She possessed a most delightful wit. She was inquisitive. Passionate.

DIMMESDALE. There is a... femininity about me... that appeals sometimes to children.

CHILLINGWORTH. And so young. She was a child herself when she married me. I took from her eagerly. Selfishly. She gave to me... well, who can say what the source of her generosity was.

DIMMESDALE. But I don't care much for children. They sweat. They're untidy.

CHILLINGWORTH. Perhaps it was her Mediterranean nature—

DIMMESDALE. Native. Her native nature.

CHILLINGWORTH. I beg your pardon.

DIMMESDALE. Your wife. She was a native. Of the woods beyond Boston.

CHILLINGWORTH. She was not.

DIMMESDALE. Yes. Yes, you've told me. A thousand times.

CHILLINGWORTH. No. I did not.

DIMMESDALE. Roger, I... well... I wouldn't have thought a man could confuse the facts of his wife's background.

CHILLINGWORTH. She fucked me with astonishing abandon and despised every minute of it. I confuse nothing.

(A silence. CHILLINGWORTH opens his black bag, removes a vial of liquid and sets it down on the ground between himself and DIMMESDALE. A silence. DIMMESDALE picks up the vial, sniffs at it.)

DIMMESDALE. It has a bitter odor.

CHILLINGWORTH. Have you never tasted a woman, Arthur?

DIMMESDALE. Women... trust me.

CHILLINGWORTH. You might not be so mysteriously ill. If you kept company with women.

DIMMESDALE. Shall I drink this now?

CHILLINGWORTH. But you've lost faith in my medicines. Why take this one?

DIMMESDALE. I have nothing to lose.

CHILLINGWORTH. Spoken like a man of science, Arthur. Like a man who's had a woman.

DIMMESDALE. This is new, this tonic. Where does it come from?

CHILLINGWORTH. Drink it and see.

(A beat, and DIMMESDALE drinks.)

CHILLINGWORTH. Trust is an odious virtue, Arthur. I'd rather be desired by women than have their trust. *(Beat.)* The tonic was prepared from a weed I found on an unmarked grave.

DIMMESDALE. That is sacrilege.

CHILLINGWORTH. It's good science, Arthur.

DIMMESDALE. How could you treat me with... with—

CHILLINGWORTH. Unknown properties?

DIMMESDALE. You could have killed me with it.

CHILLINGWORTH. I had faith in the weed, Arthur. In its properties. You said you had nothing to lose.

DIMMESDALE. You shut me out. You always have.

CHILLINGWORTH. My theory is this: The weed grows from a secret buried in the heart of the man who rests in that unmarked grave.

DIMMESDALE. How do you know it's a man?

CHILLINGWORTH. Men have secrets.

DIMMESDALE. And women do not?

CHILLINGWORTH. Women may have secrets. But men keep them.

DIMMESDALE. That's a dubious theory, Roger.

CHILLINGWORTH. How would you know? You don't put much faith in scientific theory.

DIMMESDALE. We are such good friends. Don't do this.

CHILLINGWORTH. The tonic works already.

DIMMESDALE. I feel no difference. I remain seated in dirt.

CHILLINGWORTH. You've looked me in the eye. The first time this day.

DIMMESDALE. *(After a beat):* The sun has been bright today, Roger.

(CHILLINGWORTH takes the empty vial and puts it back into his bag.)

DIMMESDALE. I've often wondered what you keep in that bag.

CHILLINGWORTH. I keep what I need.

DIMMESDALE. And what is that? What, for instance, do you need from me?

CHILLINGWORTH. I am not inclined to heartfelt discussions, Arthur.

DIMMESDALE. But I am. I'd like to know. Please.

CHILLINGWORTH. A man burdened with a secret should especially avoid the intimacy of his physician.

DIMMESDALE. I keep no secret from you.

(CHILLINGWORTH removes another vial of liquid from his bag and holds it out to DIMMESDALE.)

CHILLINGWORTH. Drink up, Arthur.

(A silence. DIMMESDALE reaches for the vial as lights fade from them, and lights rise on HESTER and PEARL at the edge of the woods. HESTER carries a pair of exquisitely embroidered gloves.)

PEARL. I'm fond of decomposition. Transformation. Leaves. Small animals. I collect these things. Hester becomes a legend. The myth of her letter grows into spectacle. As if she and it burn a streak of conscience through the dense New England psyche. Hester embroiders and gains renown. I collect more trophies. Hester keeps nothing. She donates everything to the poor. I have nightmares. Hester transforms. My nightmares begin and end with the letter *A*.

HESTER. Why do you stand so long at the edge of wood, Pearl?

PEARL. I'm waiting for the dark man.

HESTER. There is no dark man.

PEARL. Mistress Hibbins says he can take me places.

HESTER. I take you places.

PEARL. You take me to the scaffold.

HESTER. That was long ago.

PEARL. Take me again.

HESTER. There are better places to go, Pearl.

PEARL. Where?

HESTER. I don't know. Exactly.

PEARL. You said there were better places. Tell me where they are.

HESTER. How would I know, child? I've never been anywhere better.

PEARL. Don't you want to go?

HESTER. Not especially.

PEARL. In a better place, people would look at us more.

HESTER. I worry about you, Pearl.

PEARL. People look at us when we're on the scaffold.

HESTER. That doesn't make it a better place.

PEARL. I like to be looked at.

HESTER. Nobody decent likes to be looked at.

PEARL. Are you decent?

HESTER. I'm weary.

PEARL. If you don't like to be looked at, then why do you wear such a pretty letter?

HESTER. Gather flowers, Pearl. Play.

PEARL. Play with me.

HESTER. I can't. I'm waiting.

PEARL. Who has died?

HESTER. No one's died, child.

PEARL. When people die, you make things for them. Dresses. Gloves. Whose gloves are those?

HESTER. These are Governor Bellingham's gloves, Pearl. We're waiting for him.

PEARL. Is he my father?

HESTER. No. He's the Governor.

PEARL. Who is my father?

HESTER. You're fatherless.

PEARL. Mistress Hibbins says everybody's got a father.

HESTER. Mistress Hibbins is wrong. Some people are gifts. You are God's gift to me, Pearl. Kiss me. Come here and kiss your mother.

PEARL. I'd rather kiss my father.

HESTER. That is not possible, Pearl. Don't be sad. Let me hold you.

PEARL. I'm not sad. I'm waiting for my father.

HESTER. It's cold, Pearl. Come here and keep me warm.

PEARL. What's a whore?

HESTER. *(A beat.)* Sometimes I shudder at the thought of you, Pearl.

PEARL. Are you a whore?

HESTER. You are my flesh. Kiss me.

PEARL. You're boring.

(PEARL gathers burrs from the wood.)

HESTER. I'm your mother. I don't have to interest you.

PEARL. Why do people look away from you?

HESTER. You rarely call me mother anymore. Why is that?

PEARL. People didn't look away from you when we were on the scaffold.

HESTER. People are strange. Do you love me, Pearl?

PEARL. You ask a lot of questions.

HESTER. *(A beat.)* The Governor will come soon.

PEARL. I'll love you if you play with me.

HESTER. Do what you will, child.

(PEARL throws the burrs at HESTER'S letter, one at a time. Occasionally, a burr sticks to HESTER'S dress or to the letter. HESTER remains quite still throughout the following scene with PEARL.)

PEARL. You be me, and I'll be my father.

HESTER. I don't like this game.

PEARL I saw the minister yesterday. I smiled at him and he put his hand over his heart.

HESTER. You never smile at anybody. Stop this game now, Pearl.

PEARL. Why does the minister keep his hand over his heart?

HESTER. Do not test me, Pearl.

PEARL. But why? Is he very sick?

HESTER. He has much to think about.

PEARL. The why doesn't he keep his hand over his head?

HESTER. I don't recognize you sometimes. I look at you

and I don't see anything that's mine.

PEARL. Hester. Look how the burrs stick to you.

(GOVERNOR BELLINGHAM enters.)

PEARL. The dark man is here.

(PEARL goes to HESTER.)

BELLINGHAM. What was that, child?

HESTER. You startled her, Governor. That is all.

BELLINGHAM. I'm sorry. It is not my practice to startle children.

PEARL. Why not?

BELLINGHAM. Children don't like to be startled.

PEARL. I do.

HESTER. I... brought your gloves, Governor, in the hope that you might pass this way.

BELLINGHAM. That is good of you, Mistress Prynne. Though I would have gladly made the trip to your cottage to fetch them.

PEARL. We don't like guests.

(CHILLINGWORTH and DIMMESDALE enter. CHILLINGWORTH carries his bag, as usual.)

PEARL. *(To CHILLINGWORTH.)* Hello. You're the ugliest man I've ever seen.

HESTER. Pearl. Mind your manners.

BELLINGHAM. Really, Mistress Prynne, your child is most offensive.

CHILLINGWORTH. Never mind, Governor. The child and I understand each other. Truth cannot offend. Isn't that right, Pearl?

PEARL. Did you meet the dark man in the woods?

(CHILLINGWORTH laughs. DIMMESDALE'S a bit woozy.)

BELLINGHAM. Reverend Dimmesdale--let me help you.
DIMMESDALE. I'm fine. Really. We've had quite a long walk.

(BELLINGHAM assists DIMMESDALE.)

PEARL. Mother, is the minister dying?
HESTER. Go off and play, Pearl. I must speak to these men now.
PEARL. There's nowhere to go.
CHILLINGWORTH. *(To PEARL.)* Boston is full of possibilities, child.
PEARL. How many possibilities?
CHILLINGWORTH. Why don't you go count them?

(A beat, and PEARL wanders off to the prison doorway. She methodically picks petals from the rosebush surrounding the door.)

CHILLINGWORTH. *(To HESTER.)* Delightful child. Forthright.
HESTER. Governor Bellingham, we must discuss a matter of some urgency.
BELLINGHAM. Can't it wait, Mistress Prynne? The Reverend is in a state of considerable distress.

HESTER. So am I.

CHILLINGWORTH. *(To DIMMESDALE.)* Perhaps we should be getting on, Arthur.

HESTER. Stay. This need not be a private discussion.

(DIMMESDALE reaches out to HESTER. She stands stock-still.)

DIMMESDALE. Your dress, Mistress Prynne. There's a burr on your dress.

(A beat, then DIMMESDALE picks the burr off her dress. HESTER remains quite still.)

DIMMESDALE. Mister Chillingworth uses burrs sometimes. For his tonics.

(DIMMESDALE gives the burr to CHILLINGWORTH.)

CHILLINGWORTH. An excellent specimen, Arthur. Thank you. *(To HESTER.)* The Reverend is most concerned with the state of his health. Sometimes, he can think of nothing else.

(A silence.)

BELLINGHAM. What is this matter of urgency, Mistress Prynne?

HESTER. I understand you mean to take my child from me.

BELLINGHAM. I see. And how have you come to... understand... this?

CHILLINGWORTH. *(Opening his bag.)* Would anyone care for a whiskey? I find it most refreshing in the afternoon. *(A beat.)* No? Well. To your collective health, then.

(CHILLINGWORTH drinks from a small bottle.)

HESTER. There is much gossip in the marketplace. Women are indiscreet.

BELLINGHAM. Which women?

HESTER. Let's not digress. You must not take Pearl away from me, Governor.

BELLINGHAM. This is not the time, Mistress Prynne. Nor the place.

HESTER. This is the only time and place I have.

BELLINGHAM. There are questions.

HESTER. I can answer any question.

BELLINGHAM. I think not, Mistress Prynne. We feel you are not the appropriate person to instill the child with sufficient Christian foundation.

HESTER. Who is "we"?

BELLINGHAM. That is irrelevant.

HESTER. You said "we." Name these men.

BELLINGHAM. There is... myself. And several others.

HESTER. Reverend. Is this true?

DIMMESDALE. You mustn't question the Governor's authority, Hester.

BELLINGHAM. It is my responsibility, Mistress Prynne, to make decisions for the good of the community.

HESTER. I am the child's mother, Governor. I couldn't be more appropriate to raise her.

BELLINGHAM. Ordinarily, I would agree with you. You've

lost your way, Mistress Prynne. We must see to it that the child doesn't lose hers.

HESTER. Children lose their way all the time. That is their nature. Do you agree, Reverend?

DIMMESDALE. I suppose. It happens.

BELLINGHAM. We fear for her soul.

HESTER. And do you not fear for mine?

BELLINGHAM. Yours was lost long ago, Mistress Prynne.

HESTER. You would not take my punishment from me, would you?

BELLINGHAM. Only our Lord can revoke punishment.

HESTER. The child is my punishment.

BELLINGHAM. *(A beat.)* Allow me to question her.

HESTER. She is unused to questioning.

BELLINGHAM. I must be allowed to assess the quality of her upbringing. Call the child, Mistress Prynne.

(A silence.)

DIMMESDALE. Do not deny his request, Hester. Call the child.

(PEARL goes to HESTER.)

HESTER. I already have.

BELLINGHAM. I heard no call.

CHILLINGWORTH. I did.

HESTER. Pearl, the Governor will ask you some questions. You will answer with consideration.

PEARL. Must I?

BELLINGHAM. Now, child. Do not be afraid.

PEARL. Are you evil?

BELLINGHAM. Of course I'm not.

PEARL. Why, then, would I fear you?

BELLINGHAM. Do you know what evil is?

PEARL. Boston is evil.

BELLINGHAM. But that is preposterous child. You live in Boston.

PEARL. I know.

BELLINGHAM. Do you know who made you, child?

PEARL. I wasn't made.

BELLINGHAM. Oh? Then where do you come from?

PEARL. I was plucked from the bush of wild roses that frames the prison door.

BELLINGHAM. This is outrageous, Mistress Prynne. I have heard enough. She must be taken from you at once.

HESTER. Never. Never will you take her, Governor. I would sooner kill—

DIMMESDALE. Hester. Hester, calm yourself. *(Beat.)* I have much to say, Governor.

BELLINGHAM. A man in your condition, Reverend Dimmesdale, would best save his energy for a more spiritually... fruitful matter.

DIMMESDALE. There is nothing more fruitful than a mother's love for her child, Governor.

CHILLINGWORTH. *(To HESTER.)* Indeed. I wonder where this might lead.

DIMMESDALE. The girl should not be separated from her mother.

BELLINGHAM. But surely, Reverend, when the mother is unfit—

DIMMESDALE. Tell me, Governor, which of Boston's

mothers would be fit for this child?

BELLINGHAM. I... hadn't thought of any one in particular.

DIMMESDALE. Hester understands her nature better than any of us. She nurtures the child. She loves her well. Could you love Pearl, Governor? Could the women of Boston love her?

BELLINGHAM. I'm sure we... could learn... to love her. It is our duty as Christians.

DIMMESDALE. It may be your duty. But it is not your right. It is Hester Prynne's right to love Pearl. The child is Hester's living caution.

BELLINGHAM. I had not considered this previously, Reverend.

DIMMESDALE. Consider it now. We cannot know the extent of this woman's suffering. Do not add to it.

CHILLINGWORTH. *(To HESTER.)* He's eloquent, no?

BELLINGHAM. *(A beat.)* Once again, Mistress Prynne, our good minister has reminded me of the necessity for compassion. Very well. I may regret this decision, however, the child may remain with you. For now.

HESTER. Forever.

BELLINGHAM. Do not be ungrateful for my kindness, Mistress Prynne.

HESTER. I am grateful for God's kindness, Governor.

(PEARL goes to DIMMESDALE. She takes his hand and rubs it against her cheek. DIMMESDALE, at a loss for the right action, kisses her forehead. She laughs, and walks off into the woods. DIMMESDALE looks after her. HESTER holds out the gloves to BELLINGHAM.)

HESTER. Your gloves, Governor.

BELLINGHAM. *(He takes them.)* Mistress Prynne, they are... exquisite. I must pay you well for these.

HESTER. You've already paid me well today, Governor. Good day. *(She begins to exit after PEARL and stops a moment near DIMMESDALE.)* Thank you.

DIMMESDALE. It's nothing. *(A beat.)* Really.

HESTER. It's everything.

(HESTER walks off into the woods. A silence as the men look after her.)

DIMMESDALE. I don't get on well with children. Usually.

BELLINGHAM. Who does? Especially with such an odd child. Such an... old... child.

CHILLINGWORTH. Fathers do. And mothers. Parents.

DIMMESDALE. You've uncanny perceptions, Roger. For a man without a family.

CHILLINGWORTH. You are my family, Arthur.

BELLINGHAM. I pray I haven't judged the situation incorrectly. *(Beat.)* Mistress Prynne is a remarkable seamstress. These gloves. Such elegance.

CHILLINGWORTH. Mistress Prynne is an elegant woman, Governor. Quite unlike her spawn.

DIMMESDALE. She is yet a child, Roger. Hold your judgment.

BELLINGHAM. There is something elusive about that child.

CHILLINGWORTH. Perhaps by analyzing the child's nature carefully, one might uncover the secret of her paternity.

DIMMESDALE. Children are not replications of their parents.

CHILLINGWORTH. No. But they are cast from their shadows.

BELLINGHAM. Well, then. My sister casts a long shadow, gentlemen, and I must get back to her.

CHILLINGWORTH. Is Mistress Hibbins unwell?

BELLINGHAM. That, Mister Chillingworth, is a question to which I've given considerable thought. *(Beat.)* She is greatly agitated of late. She sits by the window and waits. For what, I cannot say.

DIMMESDALE. She might benefit from one of Mister Chillingworth's tonics.

BELLINGHAM. My sister needs a noose, Reverend. Not a tonic. Good day, gentlemen.

(BELLINGHAM exits.)

CHILLINGWORTH. A harsh man. Full of regret. Bitterness. Such leadership potential.

DIMMESDALE. I've never known you to drink, Roger.

CHILLINGWORTH. I drink when I'm thirsty. Do you?

DIMMESDALE. My thirsts are uncomplicated.

CHILLINGWORTH. You look thin, Arthur. Hungry.

DIMMESDALE. I'm fasting.

CHILLINGWORTH. Fasting will not assist your recovery.

DIMMESDALE. It cleanses.

CHILLINGWORTH. There are other methods of cleansing. Confession, for instance.

DIMMESDALE. Confession aids in spiritual cleansing, Roger.

CHILLINGWORTH. Perhaps your illness has its roots in the spiritual.

DIMMESDALE. If that is true, then God will have his way with me.

CHILLINGWORTH. You are simpleminded, Arthur.

DIMMESDALE. You are out of your depth in matters of the spirit, Roger.

CHILLINGWORTH. I have lived long. Seen much.

DIMMESDALE. You know not my heart.

CHILLINGWORTH. I may not know it. But I have examined it well.

DIMMESDALE. I am your only patient.

CHILLINGWORTH. You need is greatest.

DIMMESDALE. You blind yourself to the needs of others, Roger. Look around you.

CHILLINGWORTH. I once looked after the needs of another. *(A beat.)* Obsession has its uses.

DIMMESDALE. You should remarry.

CHILLINGWORTH. Share a whiskey with me, Arthur.

(CHILLINGWORTH drinks from his bottle, offers it to DIMMESDALE, who doesn't take it.)

DIMMESDALE. Why have you never remarried? Surely a man of your... knowledge... would have an easy time of it with women.

CHILLINGWORTH. I prefer books to women.

DIMMESDALE. You have much to offer. You've given me my life.

CHILLINGWORTH. And yet you do not trust me with your secrets.

DIMMESDALE. I swear to you, I keep nothing back.

CHILLINGWORTH. I know. *(Beat.)* What I wouldn't give for a good library.

DIMMESDALE. Books had a purpose for me once. But now they seem increasingly superfluous.

(CHILLINGWORTH grabs DIMMESDALE.)

CHILLINGWORTH. Touch me.

(A silence. DIMMESDALE, not certain of his function, touches CHILLINGWORTH'S face, caresses it.)

DIMMESDALE. I touch you and I am full of revulsion.

CHILLINGWORTH. My heart, Arthur. Touch my heart.

DIMMESDALE. I cannot bear to touch anyone other than myself.

CHILLINGWORTH. Do me this favor. Learn.

(DIMMESDALE places his hand over CHILLINGWORTH'S heart.)

CHILLINGWORTH. It is cold, Arthur. Someone bears responsibility for this.

DIMMESDALE. You must bare your heart in order to heal it.

(CHILLINGWORTH removes DIMMESDALE'S hand from his heart and places it on DIMMESDALE'S heart.)

CHILLINGWORTH. Heed your own advice.

DIMMESDALE. Life is meant to be lived with others. Be fruitful and multiply.

CHILLINGWORTH. I share my life with you.

DIMMESDALE. That isn't the same.

CHILLINGWORTH. What woman would have me.

(Silence. CHILLINGWORTH takes a long swig of whiskey. He packs the bottle back into his bag and begins to exit.)

DIMMESDALE. Don't leave me here. I... cannot be alone.

CHILLINGWORTH. We all stand alone before God.

DIMMESDALE. Do not abandon me, Roger.

CHILLINGWORTH. *(A beat.)* Be fruitful and multiply. Indeed.

(CHILLINGWORTH exits. Lights up on PEARL at the prison door.)

DIMMESDALE. I am paralyzed.

PEARL. And so the minister, unable to move, hallucinates.

(Suddenly it is night, and growing darker by the minute.)

DIMMESDALE. I am undone undone oh what my heart yearns to be free of my tongue fights to keep what evil do I perpetrate what sin do I conceal I must cleanse I must cleanse myself alone I stand alone my past is past is my own is Hester is is is confession I am rooted oh Roger I am forsaken I am unclean uncleansed I SIN I AM MY SIN MY LOVE I AM UNDONE.

(Lights up on the balcony. BRACKETT, HIBBINS and BELLINGHAM applaud.)

BELLINGHAM. Well done, Reverend Dimmesdale.

BRACKETT. No finer words have passed his lips.

BELLINGHAM. He's an angel. An angel on earth.

HIBBINS. Heartbreaker. That's what he is. Makes me tingle all over, he does.

DIMMESDALE. I... I wrong you all. I am not what I appear to be.

BELLINGHAM. Such extraordinary honesty. It's too much, Reverend. You slay me.

DIMMESDALE. What words are these, what thoughts?

BRACKETT. An example to us all. A real gem.

DIMMESDALE. I am a liar. A hypocrite.

HIBBINS. Ooooo. Stop. Stop. You make me hot, sweetheart.

BRACKETT. I feel a swoon coming on.

BELLINGHAM. Bravo. You great big saint, you.

(Lights down on the balcony. DIMMESDALE cries out.)

DIMMESDALE. IT IS NOT SO.

PEARL. Noooo. But: Confession makes their hearts grow fonder. And so the minister takes a walk.

(DIMMESDALE walks towards the scaffold. HESTER appears beside PEARL at the prison door.)

PEARL. Look. The dark man's come from the woods.

HESTER. There's no one ahead of us, Pearl.

PEARL. He walks with his hand over his heart.

(PEARL laughs. DIMMESDALE stops.)

DIMMESDALE. Who's there?
HESTER. What are these visions, child? Why do you see that which I cannot fathom?
DIMMESDALE. Who's there? Who witnesses this?
PEARL. He's calling us. Like music. Listen.

(PEARL laughs.)

DIMMESDALE. DO NOT TORMENT ME.

(DIMMESDALE lets loose a terrible cry. He collapses. Lights up on the balcony to reveal MISTRESS HIBBINS and BELLINGHAM dressed for bed.)

BELLINGHAM. Sister. I thought I heard a cry.
HIBBINS. My master commands me to ride with him to-night. See him there, at the scaffold?
BELLINGHAM. It's a wolf. A wild animal. Go back to sleep.
HIBBINS. I'm coming, master. Wait for me.
BELLINGHAM. Sometimes, sister, I despise you. *(A beat.)* Come to bed.

(Lights down on the balcony. PEARL steps nearer to the scaffold. DIMMESDALE sees her.)

DIMMESDALE. Child. Pearl.
PEARL. Will you bring me to the woods, minister?

HESTER. You are always straying from me, child. Stay with me. Stay.

DIMMESDALE. Hester. Is it you? Let me see you.

HESTER. Arthur. I am here.

DIMMESDALE. I did not wish for you to see me here. Like this.

PEARL. The minister has fallen, mama.

HESTER. Then we shall help him.

PEARL. Why? He doesn't help us.

HESTER. The night holds much danger, Pearl.

(HESTER goes to help DIMMESDALE. From the moment they touch, neither pays any real attention to PEARL or to what she is saying.)

DIMMESDALE. You mustn't touch me, Hester.

HESTER. I have wanted nothing else.

DIMMESDALE. I am not worthy.

PEARL. We watched a man die tonight, minister.

HESTER. The worth of my passion cannot be measured.

(DIMMESDALE stands.)

DIMMESDALE. No. Come no closer. You are an apparition.

PEARL. We sat by his bed. Hester wiped sweat from his forehead and then he died. I thought there would be more to it. I closed his eyes when nobody was watching.

HESTER. Touch me. See if I'm real.

(HESTER holds out her hand to DIMMESDALE. A bell begins to strike midnight.)

DIMMESDALE. I walked this night to release my burden of guilt. And everyone's asleep.

HESTER. Take my hand.

(The bell continues to toll. DIMMESDALE holds HESTER'S hand. A silence.)

PEARL. The dead man was warm. I held his hand for a long time after he'd died and he didn't go cold. I thought he might freeze. But he just kept... lying there.

HESTER. I've missed you.

DIMMESDALE. You mustn't.

HESTER. Miss me, Arthur. Please.

DIMMESDALE. Stand with me tonight. On the scaffold.

HESTER. All this would not go for nought if you would just... miss me.

DIMMESDALE. Ascend with me, Hester. *(As if he suddenly remembers PEARL is there.)* And the child, as well. We will stand together this night, Pearl. Pearl, ascend with us.

PEARL. Will we fly?

DIMMESDALE. No child. We will climb.

(DIMMESDALE holds his hand out to PEARL. She comes very near to him as if to inspect his hand. She ignores it and steps onto the scaffold.)

DIMMESDALE. She hates me.

HESTER. You're a stranger to her.

DIMMESDALE. I cannot see you, Hester. My sight is gone. Don't leave me here.

HESTER. *(A beat.)* I have always loved your smell, Arthur.

(HESTER leads DIMMESDALE onto the scaffold. The bell continues to toll. HESTER joins hands with DIMMESDALE, who joins hands with PEARL. DIMMESDALE stands between the women. They stand together in silence. It seems to grow darker and darker.)

PEARL. Is it midnight, Hester?

HESTER. It's midnight.

PEARL. The clock strikes many times more than twelve.

HESTER. Then time has stopped.

PEARL. Will you stand with us here tomorrow, minister, at noon, in the sunshine?

DIMMESDALE. Not tomorrow, child.

PEARL. When?

DIMMESDALE. Not tomorrow.

PEARL. But when, minister, will you stand with Hester and I in the sunshine?

DIMMESDALE. On Judgment Day, child, we will all stand together in daylight.

(A magnificent comet lights up the sky. It is preternaturally bright and reveals CHILLINGWORTH standing at the edge of the scaffold. DIMMESDALE and HESTER do not notice him. They look up to chart the course of the comet. PEARL slowly raises a finger to point at CHILLINGWORTH. He moves toward her. It becomes unbearably bright.)

BLACKOUT

ACT II

(Lights up on DIMMESDALE in the graveyard. He is on his hands and knees, his clothing caked with dirt. He crawls about pulling weeds from the graves. He examines each weed carefully, as if he's searching for one in particular. The search is methodical rather than frantic. PEARL appears at the prison doorway momentarily, watches DIMMESDALE, smiles, plucks a rose from the doorway and disappears into the woods. BRACKETT enters the graveyard. He carries a glove. He watches DIMMESDALE for a moment before speaking. DIMMESDALE continues to pull weeds throughout this exchange.)

BRACKETT. I could fetch the gardener, sir.

DIMMESDALE. Please. Don't call me sir. I'm not your master.

BRACKETT. I mean no disrespect. *(A beat.)* I found a glove this morning.

DIMMESDALE. Wear it well, Master Brackett.

BRACKETT. It isn't mine.

DIMMESDALE. It isn't a sin to find a glove and keep it, man. Anybody could have dropped it.

BRACKETT. It's your glove, sir.

DIMMESDALE. For God's sake, Brackett. I am your minister, not your captain. Call me by my name

BRACKETT. I found it on the scaffold this morning. *(A beat.)* I'm ashamed to say I don't know your name, Reverend.

DIMMESDALE. *(Stops pulling weeds.)* Arthur. My name is Arthur.

BRACKETT. Funny the things we don't learn over time.

DIMMESDALE. Yes.

BRACKETT. My name is Julius, but you wouldn't know it. Even my wife calls me Brackett. I don't mind.

DIMMESDALE. Yes.

BRACKETT. Last night she called me Julius. She woke me to see the portent. But I was so surprised to hear my own name, I forgot to look. *(A beat.)* I couldn't call you by your name, Reverend. Wouldn't be right.

(DIMMESDALE goes back to pulling weeds.)

BRACKETT. Did you see the portent, Reverend?

DIMMESDALE. No.

BRACKETT. It lit up the town, it did. The letter *A* streaking across the sky.

DIMMESDALE. How do you know it was there?

BRACKETT. My wife told me. And this morning, in the marketplace, it was all anybody could talk about.

DIMMESDALE. But you didn't see it.

BRACKETT. No. But others saw it.

DIMMESDALE. You're a reasonable man, Brackett. Use your common sense. You saw no portent. Therefore, there wasn't a portent.

BRACKETT. But Reverend, the whole town says—

DIMMESDALE. There is no proof of this portent. There isn't a trace of it. If you cannot point your finger to something it does not exist.

(An awkward silence.)

BRACKETT. General Winthrop passed on last night.

DIMMESDALE. What do you mean, passed on? He died, Brackett. He is dead.

BRACKETT. Well. I expect that's true.

DIMMESDALE. Passed on. What does that mean, Brackett? Can you touch something that's passed on?

BRACKETT. I mean no disrespect.

DIMMESDALE. Will you please stop groveling. Go on. Leave me. I have work.

(Silence. DIMMESDALE continues searching for weeds. He stops when he realizes BRACKETT hasn't yet gone.)

DIMMESDALE. Is there something else? Perhaps another mind-numbing question of conscience?

BRACKETT. Your glove, sir.

(BRACKETT holds out the glove to DIMMESDALE. A silence.)

BRACKETT. I thought it must be the devil's work, sir, finding your glove on the scaffold. But since I didn't see the devil put it there himself, I guess he didn't do it.

DIMMESDALE. *(Taking the glove from Brackett.)* I haven't been well.

BRACKETT. There was a chill in the air last night. Not at all like summer. They say the *A* in the sky stood for angel. And that our Lord was warming the way to heaven for General Winthrop's journey. *(A beat.)* Let me send for the gardener, Reverend.

DIMMESDALE. You know not why I search here, nor what I search for.

BRACKETT. It's not for me to question you, Reverend.

DIMMESDALE. Question me, Brackett.

BRACKETT. Reverend, really—

DIMMESDALE. I beg you. Please. You know nothing about me.

BRACKETT. You don't know anything about me, either.

DIMMESDALE. I know that you are Julius Brackett, married some thirty years to Charlotte. I know that your four sons love you well. I know that sometimes you imagine yourself back in Bristol, where you would smoke pipes and drink all day. *(A beat.)* What do you know about me?

BRACKETT. I know your name.

DIMMESDALE. That is not enough. Question me.

(An awkward silence.)

BRACKETT. Well, then, What are you doing out here?

DIMMESDALE. Pulling weeds. Ask another question.

BRACKETT. I... was that a good question to ask?

DIMMESDALE. Excellent question, Brackett. Go on.

BRACKETT. *(He thinks hard.)* Why are you pulling weeds?

DIMMESDALE. To get to the root. Ask me more.

BRACKETT. Reverend, I can't. I... I'll fetch you a doctor.

(DIMMESDALE grabs BRACKETT by his lapels.)

DIMMESDALE. I'm done with doctors. No doctors. They cannot cure my illness. They cannot find its roots.

(A silence. DIMMESDALE releases BRACKETT and sinks to the ground.)

DIMMESDALE. I'm covered in dirt.
BRACKETT. Nothing a hot bath won't cure.
DIMMESDALE. I'm a mess, Brackett. Look at this mess.
BRACKETT. Nobody here to care about the mess.
DIMMESDALE. Yes. Well. At least I have my glove.

(DIMMESDALE puts the glove on.)

BRACKETT. I'll take you home, Reverend.
DIMMESDALE. I'm unclean.
BRACKETT. Well... you don't notice it. Much.
DIMMESDALE. You're a good man, Brackett.
BRACKETT. And so are you, sir.

(BRACKETT helps DIMMESDALE to his feet.)

DIMMESDALE. I don't have far to go.
BRACKETT. Just up the hill, isn't it?
DIMMESDALE. Just up the hill.

(They begin to walk. DIMMESDALE nearly collapses. He can't go on.)

DIMMESDALE. It's no use. Leave me. The journey is not far. The journey... Don't leave me, Brackett. The journey... is...
BRACKETT. You baptized my sons, sir.
DIMMESDALE. Julius. Don't go.

BRACKETT. I won't leave you, Arthur.

(BRACKETT hoists DIMMESDALE over his shoulders, pig-gyback style. He begins to walk. Lights up on HESTER, who stands at the edge of the scaffold. She watches the men leave. Lights fade from DIMMESDALE and BRACKETT. Lights up on CHILLINGWORTH, who enters the graveyard from the woods. He surveys the mess and begins to gather the weeds that DIMMESDALE has pulled. HESTER enters the graveyard. Silence, as CHILLINGWORTH works.)

CHILLINGWORTH. Is it true, Mistress Prynne, that Governor Bellingham means to remove the punishment of your scarlet letter?

HESTER. I have heard no such thing.

CHILLINGWORTH. But I think it is true. You have done such good work for the poor and the infirm, Hester. Our community need reward you for your service.

HESTER. Don't patronize me.

CHILLINGWORTH. The Governor had his doubts. But you have a formidable ally in the Reverend Dimmesdale.

HESTER. Were I worthy, the letter would drop from me of its own accord.

CHILLINGWORTH. Your religious fervor worries me, Hester.

HESTER. What have you done to him?

CHILLINGWORTH. *(Indicates the mess of the graveyard.)* Undoubtedly the work of malicious children. Such waste.

HESTER. His eyes. I loved the way they took in the whole of me.

CHILLINGWORTH. But then, children are born to be malicious.

HESTER. I won't witness his destruction.

CHILLINGWORTH. Ah, but you have a child. A girl whose very nature defies analysis. Why is that?

HESTER. We must talk.

CHILLINGWORTH. My time is short, Hester. And there is much to do before I rest.

HESTER. You're fortunate to rest at all, given the great weight on your conscience.

CHILLINGWORTH. I sleep easily, Hester. If you disturb my work, there will be complications. *(A beat.)* I have done more for him than any man.

HESTER. Then perhaps you can do no more.

CHILLINGWORTH. But I have not done all that I can. *(A beat.)* I miss our talks, Hester. They invigorate me.

HESTER. I can keep your identity from him no longer.

(CHILLINGWORTH holds out a weed to HESTER.)

CHILLINGWORTH. Do you know what this is?

HESTER. Do not ignore me, husband.

CHILLINGWORTH. This has kept him alive, Hester.

HESTER. He little values his life.

CHILLINGWORTH. His spirit is weak. But mine is strong enough for both of us.

HESTER. You've lost your spirit. Do not take what's left of his.

CHILLINGWORTH. It's been a long while since you called me husband. *(A beat.)* Come closer, Hester.

HESTER. I can pay you. Any price. I will pay it.

CHILLINGWORTH. I cannot stop what is already in motion. It is a cardinal rule of science.

HESTER. You can alter the nature of the motion.

CHILLINGWORTH. What would you have me alter, Hester?

HESTER. Forgive him.

CHILLINGWORTH. Would you kneel to me?

(HESTER kneels.)

HESTER. It is done.

CHILLINGWORTH. And will you now crawl to me?

(A silence. HESTER crawls to him.)

HESTER. Forgive him.

CHILLINGWORTH. And will you kiss my feet?

HESTER. There is yet time in which to redeem yourself, Roger.

CHILLINGWORTH. Forgiveness isn't worth much to you, Hester.

(HESTER kisses CHILLINGWORTH'S feet.)

CHILLINGWORTH. The things we do for love. *(A beat.)* Lick my boots.

HESTER. I betrayed you. But I was never cruel.

CHILLINGWORTH. You married me.

HESTER. I didn't lie to you.

CHILLINGWORTH. Lick my boots. Go on.

(HESTER licks CHILLINGWORTH'S boots. Silence. CHILLINGWORTH gathers dirt into his hands.)

HESTER. The texture of his hair. His taste. His gentle touch. These things I hold dear. The sound of his voice. His eyes. His—

(CHILLINGWORTH forces dirt into HESTER'S mouth. HESTER does not resist.)

CHILLINGWORTH. *(Forcing dirt into her mouth.)* This is his touch, Hester. Touch him. This is his taste. Taste him. You are my wife, Hester. I have seen you as no other sees you and I... will... not... I WILL NOT... LET. HIM. GO.

(CHILLINGWORTH steps back, exhausted. HESTER remains on her knees.)

HESTER. My father was a fisherman who hated the sea. I left home to find land. I found Amsterdam. Canals visible through every window. I bought curtains and spent time in libraries. Met you in the stacks. My interest was music. I learned to sew and meant to write home. Tried to make love with my eyes open. You said: The possibilities are infinite. Later, you sent me here. I got off the boat and retched.

CHILLINGWORTH. The day we met, I told you a joke. You laughed. You took my hand and I recognized something which I can no longer recall.

(HESTER rises.)

HESTER. It was gratitude. Not love. Never love.

(CHILLINGWORTH begins to cry. He reaches out to her.)

CHILLINGWORTH. Hester. *(HESTER is silent. PEARL emerges from the woods. She wears a necklace fashioned from burrs, which spells out the letter* A. *She watches HESTER. CHILLINGWORTH takes a handkerchief from his pocket and wipes dirt from HESTER'S face.)* What have I wrought?

HESTER. *(Stopping him.)* I can no longer close my eyes, Roger. *(CHILLINGWORTH neatly folds the handkerchief and holds it out to HESTER. She takes it and exits the graveyard. HESTER notices PEARL. Silence. HESTER begins to clean her face with the handkerchief. Lights fade from CHILLINGWORTH.)* Take it off, Pearl.

PEARL. You're filthy, Hester. Have you been playing in the graveyard?

HESTER. Remove it. Now. Why won't you call me mother?

PEARL. Why does the ugly doctor cry, Hester?

HESTER. Because there is nothing else to do. *(A beat. She's done wiping her face.)* Why do you disrespect me so?

PEARL. I met a wolf in the woods. It bowed its head so I could pet it.

(HESTER removes PEARL'S necklace.)

HESTER. Do you know why I wear the scarlet letter?

PEARL. The doctor is very smart. Ask him.

HESTER. I wear it because I like its gold thread, Pearl.

PEARL. Mistress Hibbins says it's the dark man's mark on you.

HESTER. *(Considers her response.)* I met the dark man long ago, Pearl. And the letter is his mark. I was allowed to meet him once and not again.

PEARL. If you met the dark man, so will I.

HESTER. I fear you've met him already.

PEARL. *(Takes back the necklace from HESTER.)* I want to be just like you.

HESTER. You know not what you say.

PEARL. *(Puts the necklace back on.)* Mine is prettier.

HESTER. Child. Have you no sadness?

(PEARL takes the handkerchief from HESTER and wipes some dirt away from HESTER'S face.)

PEARL. You missed a spot.

HESTER I should have drowned you at birth.

(HESTER walks off towards the woods. Lights up to reveal DIMMESDALE in the midst of the vast forest. He sits upon a rock. He holds a bouquet of wild flowers.)

PEARL. And so because there is nothing left for her to do, Hester finally enters the woods.

(HESTER enters the forest. A beat, before she sits with DIMMESDALE upon the rock. They sit together in silence. PEARL exits.)

DIMMESDALE. I should have worn an overcoat.

HESTER. Yes. It's deceptively chilly.

DIMMESDALE. Trees can be very tall.

HESTER. When they're old.

DIMMESDALE. I wonder, do they ever stop growing?

HESTER. They grow until they're cut down.

DIMMESDALE. Are you cold? Would you like my jacket?

HESTER. No. *(A beat.)* I'm comfortable with unpredictable weather.

DIMMESDALE. Yes.

(An awkward silence.)

DIMMESDALE. I picked some flowers.

HESTER. I'm sorry I'm late.

DIMMESDALE. No. I meant... I picked them for you.

HESTER. I don't like flowers.

DIMMESDALE. Oh. I... *(A beat.)* You look well, Hester.

HESTER. *(Impatient with all the small talk.)* You don't.

DIMMESDALE. I'm fine. I'm better. Lately.

HESTER. *(Matter-of-fact.)* I'm miserable.

DIMMESDALE. Surely it's the damp air. We could go indoors.

HESTER. I'm claustrophobic.

(A silence.)

DIMMESDALE. I'm not very good at this.

HESTER. What? What aren't you very good at?

DIMMESDALE. I... don't know. Last night was...

HESTER. Last night is gone, Arthur. *(A beat.)* Why won't you look at me?

DIMMESDALE. It's so quiet here. So dark.

HESTER. I've grown old. You haven't noticed.

DIMMESDALE. Funny that a minister should fear the dark.

HESTER. When I watch Pearl sleep I sometimes see what we might have become.

DIMMESDALE. Each day I stand at the pulpit and pray that my voice will find you somewhere at peace. That you brush the child's hair and recall something of me.

HESTER. But then she wakes.

(A silence.)

DIMMESDALE. I'm not good at courtship, Hester.

HESTER. You never were.

DIMMESDALE. I know nothing about women.

HESTER. That's part of your charm.

DIMMESDALE. I blush easily. I'm afraid of the dark. I bring you gifts you despise.

HESTER. You are no use at all. *(A beat.)* But were you to look upon me now, I could invent a thousand uses for you.

(DIMMESDALE turns to look at HESTER.)

DIMMESDALE. I... don't know what to say.

HESTER. Say: Hello.

DIMMESDALE. Hello, Hester.

HESTER. Say: I have brought you some flowers.

DIMMESDALE. I have brought you some flowers.

HESTER. *(Taking the flowers from him.)* Thank you, Arthur. I love flowers. *(A beat.)* Say: Take my hand, Hester.

DIMMESDALE. Take my hand, Hester.

(HESTER takes his hand in hers. They sit in silence.)

DIMMESDALE. What do I say now?

HESTER. Say: I no longer fear the dark.

DIMMESDALE. I no longer fear the dark.

HESTER. Because I have found the place that transcends darkness.

DIMMESDALE. Because I have found the place that transcends darkness.

HESTER. And that place is with you, Hester.

DIMMESDALE. And... I cannot find that place.

HESTER. You are there, Arthur.

DIMMESDALE. No goodness comes from sin.

HESTER. I said not a thing about sin.

DIMMESDALE. I look at you and I see it all around us.

HESTER Then close your eyes.

(DIMMESDALE closes his eyes.)

DIMMESDALE. We never talked like this. Then.

HESTER. We had much to do.

DIMMESDALE. Your hands are rough.

HESTER. They're greatly experienced.

DIMMESDALE. My hands shame me. Unblemished as a child's.

HESTER. Depends on the child.

DIMMESDALE. I have wronged you, Hester.

HESTER. You saved us once. Save us again.

DIMMESDALE. How can I save you when I cannot save myself?

HESTER. Open your eyes, Arthur.

(DIMMESDALE opens his eyes.)

HESTER. Describe what you see.

DIMMESDALE. A vision which I dare not touch.

HESTER. *(Again, she is impatient and must coax his answers, as if dealing with a child.)* No, Arthur. Use your charm.

DIMMESDALE. I touch you and my voice is lost.

HESTER. Then there is nothing more to say.

(A beat, and HESTER kisses DIMMESDALE. He accidentally bites her lip. He jumps back.)

HESTER. You've drawn blood.

DIMMESDALE. It's dripped onto your bosom.

HESTER. *(A joke.)* Good. No one will notice it.

DIMMESDALE. Everything I touch turns red.

HESTER. Then kiss it away. *(Beat.)* Arthur. Whatever else has been between us, I am your friend. Do not mistrust me.

DIMMESDALE. I am friendless.

HESTER. Don't be maudlin. It's tiresome.

DIMMESDALE. I'm the sort who does better with enemies. But even they are unavailable to me.

HESTER. And to think your naiveté once broke my heart.

DIMMESDALE. I should have brought you chocolates.

HESTER. The doctor is your enemy.

DIMMESDALE. I should have trusted my instincts and stayed indoors.

HESTER. His tonics poison you.

DIMMESDALE. Women like chocolates.

HESTER. Chillingworth is my husband.

DIMMESDALE. We might have eaten them. In silence. *(A beat.)* I know, Hester. I've always known.

HESTER. You would have liked him. Once.

DIMMESDALE. I like him now.

HESTER. He isn't even a doctor.

DIMMESDALE. He wears his deception well.

HESTER. *(Matter-of-fact.)* I can't wear mine at all anymore.

DIMMESDALE. You were always a bad liar, Hester.

HESTER. Leave him, Arthur.

DIMMESDALE. I finish what I start. It's my sole attribute.

HESTER. You'll die if you stay.

DIMMESDALE. I'll die anyway.

HESTER. We cannot sit here holding hands forever.

DIMMESDALE. Why not?

HESTER. It inevitably leads to something else.

(A silence.)

DIMMESDALE. I should have been a cobbler.

HESTER. *(Another joke.)* You're not good with your hands.

DIMMESDALE. I could learn.

(HESTER places DIMMESDALE's hands upon her breasts.)

HESTER. Then this shall be your first lesson. *(Beat.)* Help me, Arthur.

DIMMESDALE. How? How shall I help you?

HESTER. Remove the scarlet letter.

DIMMESDALE. It will not be undone.

HESTER. It's fastened with pins, Arthur. Look. *(She guides his hands to the pins and helps him to unfasten the letter. She gives him the letter.)* See how simple it is to use your hands well.

DIMMESDALE. *(Examining the letter.)* I thought it would be weightier. More... formidable. Somehow.

HESTER. *(Places his hands once again on her breasts.)* This, Arthur, is weight. Substance.

DIMMESDALE. I know not what next to do.

HESTER. Rid us of the letter.

DIMMESDALE. I... how? There is no way to erase it.

HESTER. *(Again, she must coax him into action.)* Your hands, Arthur. Use your hands.

(DIMMESDALE hesitates, then flings the letter far from them.)

DIMMESDALE. I know not my own strength.

HESTER. Lesson two: Remove my cap.

DIMMESDALE. Hester, that is too much to ask—

HESTER. I thought you always finished what you started.

(A beat. DIMMESDALE removes HESTER'S cap. She shakes loose her hair.)

DIMMESDALE. This cannot be sin.

HESTER. Whatever it is, it's waited seven years for your touch. Touch me, Arthur.

(HESTER draws DIMMESDALE into an embrace.)

DIMMESDALE. I'm shy.

HESTER. You're lying.

DIMMESDALE. Someone might see us.

HESTER. Someone's seen us already. Take me.

DIMMESDALE. Where?

HESTER. *(She laughs.)* Poor Arthur. Pick a place.

DIMMESDALE. New York.

HESTER. Think bigger.

DIMMESDALE. Rome.

HESTER. Too far.

DIMMESDALE. Paris.

HESTER. Not far enough.

DIMMESDALE. England.

HESTER. England?

DIMMESDALE. *(Attempts a joke.)* There's always England, Hester.

HESTER. I'm destined to be surrounded by water.

DIMMESDALE. When shall we go?

HESTER. Tomorrow. The Spanish Main sails to Bristol. At midnight. I've made arrangements.

DIMMESDALE. But... how could you know?

HESTER. I told you. It's my destiny.

DIMMESDALE. Is this new beginning possible, Hester? Is it true?

HESTER. Kiss me and see.

(DIMMESDALE kisses HESTER. It's a long, deep kiss.)

DIMMESDALE. Together we are free, Hester. You and I.

HESTER. And Pearl.

DIMMESDALE. Of course. Pearl.

HESTER. Give her time.

DIMMESDALE. I'm not suited to children.

HESTER. She's not an ordinary child.

DIMMESDALE. All the worse.

HESTER. Nobody is suited to children, Arthur.

DIMMESDALE. I am at such a loss to explain her.

HESTER. We cannot undo Pearl.

DIMMESDALE. Yes. The one thing I've managed to finish well.

HESTER. She will love you.

DIMMESDALE. I doubt it.

(PEARL appears at the edge of the woods.)

PEARL. Hester.

HESTER. Child. Come sit with us.

PEARL. Hester.

(DIMMESDALE brings his hand up to his heart.)

HESTER. Yes, child. It is I. Come. Sit with us.

PEARL. Hester.

(PEARL points to HESTER'S breast.)

DIMMESDALE. My breath, Hester... There is no air.

PEARL. Hester Hester THE WOODS THE WOODS THE LETTER THE WOODS Hester THE LETTER Hester—

HESTER. What is it, Pearl? What do you fear?

(But PEARL will not be silenced and continues repeating her curious chant. It is measured rather than frantic.)

DIMMESDALE. The letter. It's the letter, Hester. She does not recognize you without it. Please. Put it back.

HESTER. No, Arthur. It's not right.

DIMMESDALE. Please quiet the child, Hester. I cannot breathe.

HESTER. Pearl. Fetch the letter. *(PEARL is silent.)* Can you not hear, child?

PEARL. You get it.

HESTER. I asked you to get it for me.

PEARL. No. It's yours. You get it.

(A silence. HESTER fetches the letter and pins it to her bosom.)

HESTER. It is done. Come sit with us.

PEARL. Your hair. Do it up.

HESTER. Please, Pearl—

PEARL. The cap. Put it back. *(HESTER puts her hair up into her cap. PEARL laughs. She goes to HESTER and kisses the scarlet letter.)* I love you, mother.

HESTER. *(It is not lost on her that PEARL has called her "mother".)* Will you love the minister, as well?

PEARL. Will his hand always be at his heart?

HESTER. No, child. It is there no longer.

PEARL. Yes it is.

(HESTER looks at DIMMESDALE. His hand is over his heart.)

DIMMESDALE. I feel ill.

HESTER. Sit with the minister, Pearl.

PEARL. Why should I?

HESTER. Because I've asked nothing else of you.

(PEARL shrugs, sits with DIMMESDALE. A silence.)

DIMMESDALE. Pearl. That's a pretty name.

PEARL. How would you know? You're a minister.

DIMMESDALE. That doesn't mean I can't appreciate beauty.

PEARL. Sure it does.

DIMMESDALE. Do you... like school?

PEARL. I don't go to school.

DIMMESDALE. Every child goes to school, Pearl.

PEARL. No school will have me.

DIMMESDALE. If you don't go to school, what do you do?

PEARL. I make letters. See.

(PEARL shows DIMMESDALE her necklace.)

DIMMESDALE. That isn't funny.

PEARL. I didn't say it was.

DIMMESDALE. You're a very angry little girl.

PEARL. I'm not a girl. I'm a demon.

HESTER. Pearl, behave yourself.

DIMMESDALE. It's all right, hester. She's confused. She lacks paternal guidance.

PEARL. My father lives in the woods. Do you live in the woods?

DIMMESDALE. I live above the church, Pearl. All ministers live above churches.

PEARL. Do all ministers live above graveyards?

DIMMESDALE. No. Not all. Some.

PEARL. None but you.

DIMMESDALE. Would you like to go to school, Pearl? Would you like to go to school far from Boston?

PEARL. Mistress HIbbins is my teacher.
DIMMESDALE. She's not a proper teacher.
PEARL. You're not a proper minister. You're sick.

(A silence. DIMMESDALE kisses PEARL'S cheek. She stands.)

PEARL. Will you walk with Hester and me tomorrow?
DIMMESDALE. Yes, child. I will.
PEARL. Will you walk with us through the marketplace?
DIMMESDALE. I... cannot.

(PEARL wipes DIMMESDALE'S kiss away. She takes off her necklace and puts it around DIMMESDALE'S neck.)

PEARL. Red's your color, minister.

(PEARL walks off towards the scaffold. A silence as DIMMESDALE and HESTER regard each other. Lights face from DIMMESDALE and HESTER.)

PEARL. Contrary to my usual habit, I don't sleep at all that night. Hester, who usually sits at the window and stares into the darkness, sleeps like a baby. When I wake, she looms above me, smiling. I say, what have you got to be happy about? She says, it's a fine day for sailing. *(A beat.)* Who knows how the minister sleeps that night, or if he sleeps at all. Regardless, morning brings a bright hot sun, and summer greets the minister once again as he steps out into the marketplace.

(Lights up on DIMMESDALE at the edge of the scaffold. He eats peanuts. Lights up on HESTER at the prison doorway.

She is dressed for travel. She is packing clothing away into several bags. This is an unhurried and gentle ritual, as if she's been waiting for this moment her whole life. She watches ARTHUR, who does not see her. MISTRESS HIBBINS enters. She too does not see HESTER. She is dressed rather grandly. She stops a moment to watch DIMMESDALE eat.)

HIBBINS. How peculiar.

DIMMESDALE. Good morning, Mistress Hibbins. You look different.

HIBBINS. So do you.

DIMMESDALE. I'm eating.

HIBBINS. Good for you, Reverend.

DIMMESDALE. I'm starving.

HIBBINS. Well that's not good, is it?

DIMMESDALE. *(Finishes his peanuts.)* Have you got any food, Mistress Hibbins?

HIBBINS. I seem to be plum out of food at the moment, Reverend.

DIMMESDALE. Fruit. I'd like some fruit.

HIBBINS. You should have picked berries in the woods yesterday.

DIMMESDALE. I don't know what you're talking about.

HIBBINS. I'm ever so sorry I couldn't be with you. I had another engagement. With my brother. He can be such a handful.

DIMMESDALE. I'm sure I don't want to hear this, Mistress Hibbins.

HIBBINS. But tonight, Reverend, we will all ride again. Together.

DIMMESDALE. I really don't want to discuss this.

HIBBINS. Awwww. I understand. We can speak more freely later. When we're alone in the woods.

DIMMESDALE. Slut.

HIBBINS. I beg your pardon.

DIMMESDALE. Bitch. Whore.

HIBBINS. You shouldn't eat peanuts, minister. They clearly have a bad effect.

DIMMESDALE. Tramp. Slattern. Witch. Scum. *(A beat.)* I don't know what's come over me.

HIBBINS. I do. *(She laughs.)* Till tonight, then. *(A beat.)* Reverend.

(HIBBINS walks to the scaffold.)

DIMMESDALE. Why did I say those things? Why am I so GODDAMNED HUNGRY.

HESTER. *(More to herself than to DIMMESDALE, who can't hear her in any event.)* Hold tight, Arthur. We leave at midnight and then your hunger will be soothed. Steady. Steady now.

(GOVERNOR BELLINGHAM enters. He, too, is dressed rather grandly.)

BELLINGHAM. Did I hear you speak of our Lord, Reverend?

DIMMESDALE. Governor Bellingham. Do you have any fruit?

BELLINGHAM. Fruit?

DIMMESDALE. Nuts, then. I'll take nuts.

BELLINGHAM. You ought to take breakfast indoors.

DIMMESDALE. *(Notices BELLINGHAM'S fancy clothes.)* Is it some kind of holiday?

BELLINGHAM. You're joking, right? *(Silence.)* I see. Lack of nourishment has caused you to forget Election Day.

DIMMESDALE. You're a thief and a liar. I hope you lose.

BELLINGHAM. I didn't quite catch that, Reverend.

DIMMESDALE. I... haven't prepared a sermon.

BELLINGHAM. I'm afraid the casting of ballots will take place with or without your sermon. Good day, Reverend.

(BELLINGHAM exits to the scaffold.)

DIMMESDALE. I'm thirsty. My throat's burning. Food. I NEED FOOD. Please, please somebody...

HESTER. *(As before.)* It's not long now, Arthur. Keep calm. Boston to Halifax to St. John's. Across to Dungarven. Dungarven to Swansea, to Cardiff. To Bristol. Steady now.

(MASTER BRACKETT enters. He drinks lager.)

DIMMESDALE. Brackett. Thank Christ. *(DIMMESDALE grabs BRACKETT'S lager and drinks it in one gulp.)* Do you have any more?

BRACKETT. I had a hard enough time finding that one at this hour of the morning. *(A beat.)* I've taken to drink lately.

DIMMESDALE. I'm famished, Brackett.

BRACKETT. There's no accounting for our appetites, sir.

DIMMESDALE. I say horrible things. Think terrible thoughts.

BRACKETT. Perhaps you need a vacation, sir.

DIMMESDALE. Yes. Yes, a vacation. Is it midnight yet?

(CHILLINGWORTH enters. He does not carry his black bag.)

HESTER. *(As before.)* I swore I'd never journey across this vast ocean again. Funny how our oaths come to nought. Boston to Halifax. St. John's. Beyond. Hold tight.
CHILLINGWORTH. You look pale, Arthur.
BRACKETT. He's very hungry.
CHILLINGWORTH. Let me check for fever.

(CHILLINGWORTH attempts to check him. DIMMESDALE backs away.)

DIMMESDALE. Don't touch me.
BRACKETT. I suggested a vacation, Mister Chillingworth.
CHILLINGWORTH. Excellent idea, Brackett. In fact, I'm sailing for Bristol this evening on the Spanish Main. Perhaps the minister will join me.
DIMMESDALE. No. It cannot be.
HESTER. *(Stops packing.)* It cannot be.
CHILLINGWORTH. I booked my passage early, Arthur. You wouldn't believe the number of people wanting to catch midnight boats. *(Beat.)* Here. Let me check your pulse.
DIMMESDALE. I no longer need your medicines, Mister Chillingworth.
CHILLINGWORTH. I ran out of medicines, Arthur. See. No bag.
HESTER. It must not be.
BRACKETT. *(To CHILLINGWORTH.)* The parade's beginning, Mr. Chillingworth. Best to take a good position.

CHILLINGWORTH. Wise man, Brackett.
DIMMESDALE. What parade?

(CHILLINGWORTH and BRACKETT exit to the scaffold.)

DIMMESDALE. WHAT PARADE?
HESTER. Is it finally all for nothing?

(HIBBINS, BELLINGHAM, BRACKETT and CHILLINGWORTH all look towards the woods, as if they are following the course of something DIMMESDALE cannot see. PEARL steps up onto the scaffold and watches DIMMESDALE.)

PEARL. It's the Election Day parade, minister.
DIMMESDALE. But I have no sermon.
PEARL. That's too bad.
DIMMESDALE. I must... I must... preach.
PEARL. Too late.

(DIMMESDALE walks to the scaffold. PEARL watches his every move. The others follow the course of the phantom parade.)

DIMMESDALE. Why are they silent?
PEARL. They're not silent. You can't hear them.
HESTER. If we cannot be free of him elsewhere, we shall be free of him here.

(A bell begins to strike noon. HESTER steps forward from the prison doorway. She does not take her bags.)

DIMMESDALE. *(Finally sees her.)* Hester. Is it midnight?
HESTER. No, Arthur. It's noon.
DIMMESDALE. Oh. *(Beat.)* When do we leave?
HESTER. Midnight.
DIMMESDALE. Did you bring enough food, Hester? The trip is long and treacherous.
HESTER. There's food enough for all of us.

(The bell continues to toll.)

DIMMESDALE. Have we missed the boat, Hester?
HESTER. No, Arthur. Let me bring you there.
DIMMESDALE. I don't want to miss the boat.
HESTER. You won't.

(HESTER helps DIMMESDALE to the scaffold. CHILLINGWORTH, BRACKETT, BELLINGHAM and HIBBINS turn in unison to watch him ascend. PEARL'S attention is exclusively on DIMMESDALE.)

DIMMESDALE. Is it midnight, Hester?
HESTER. Yes, Arthur. It's midnight.

(HESTER and DIMMESDALE reach the top of the scaffold.)

DIMMESDALE. Did we miss the boat?
HESTER. No. We're on it now.
DIMMESDALE. I have much to say, Hester.
HESTER. Then speak.
DIMMESDALE. People of Boston. Hear this most unwor

thy minister. Hear... this... *(A new thought.)* Hester. Is the voyage rough?

HESTER. It's smooth, Arthur.

DIMMESDALE. When do we arrive?

HESTER. Soon, Arthur. Soon.

DIMMESDALE. People of Boston: This is my Election Day sermon.

CHILLINGWORTH. Arthur. Do not ruin your reputation.

BELLINGHAM. *(To BRACKETT.)* Is he drunk?

BRACKETT. I believe he's quite sober, sir.

DIMMESDALE. Unworthy of your affections. I am... deceived I am... undone... I undo... *(A new thought.)* The boat. Hester. It's midnight. I'm too late.

HESTER. No, Arthur. Not yet. There's time.

DIMMESDALE. Pearl. Daughter. Take my hand in the daylight.

CHILLINGWORTH. NO. YOU WILL NOT DO THIS TO ME.

BELLINGHAM. What's he talking about? Whose daughter?

BRACKETT. I believe he refers to himself, sir.

CHILLINGWORTH. NO. NO. STOP HIM.

(PEARL takes DIMMESDALE'S hand. The bell continues to toll.)

DIMMESDALE. What shall I say, Pearl?

PEARL. Whatever you'd like.

DIMMESDALE. Governor, I am weary and can no longer hide my sin. And so I take my place on this scaffold with Hester

Prynne and young Pearl. May God forgive me for not having done so seven years ago.

BELLINGHAM. What is he talking about? What sin? And why does that bell continue to chime?

HIBBINS. There's a storm in the air, brother. My master's come to call.

CHILLINGWORTH. He has escaped me.

BRACKETT. *(To BELLINGHAM.)* I believe the bell cannot be stopped, sir.

DIMMESDALE. Is it midnight yet, daughter?

PEARL. I... don't know.

HESTER. Hush, Arthur. Rest now. Rest. We'll be there soon.

DIMMESDALE. It's very hot. Fire. Is the boat on fire, daughter?

PEARL. There's no fire.

DIMMESDALE. My chest. My chest's on fire. Look. LOOK.

(DIMMESDALE bares his chest to CHILLINGWORTH, HIBBINS, BRACKETT and BELLINGHAM. Thunder. Lightening. DIMMESDALE collapses.)

PEARL. *(Finally acknowledges DIMMESDALE'S importance.)* Father.

(HESTER takes PEARL'S hand.)

PEARL. Mother.

HESTER. Hush, child. Steady. We're almost there.

CHILLINGWORTH. Arthur. You have escaped me. You are gone.

*(More thunder. It grows quite dark. Lights fade from
CHILLINGWORTH, BRACKETT, BELLINGHAM and
HIBBINS. HESTER cradles DIMMESDALE.)*

DIMMESDALE. The journey is smooth, Hester.
HESTER. Yes.
DIMMESDALE. Are we there?
HESTER. We're there.
DIMMESDALE. Pearl. Pearl, where've you gone to?
PEARL. I'm here.
DIMMESDALE. Will you kiss me, child?

(PEARL kneels to kiss DIMMESDALE.)

DIMMESDALE. Hester, she loves me well.
HESTER. She does. I do.
DIMMESDALE. I want to learn. To be. Good. With my
hands.
HESTER. You are, Arthur. You are.
DIMMESDALE. Are we there yet, Hester?
HESTER. We've been there all along.
DIMMESDALE. I... is that... I see... the woods.

*(The bell stops chiming. The thunder ceases. It begins to rain.
A smooth, fine rain. A silence. PEARL shuts
DIMMESDALE's eyes. HESTER rocks DIMMESDALE in
her arms. PEARL descends from the scaffold. HESTER lays
DIMMESDALE down onto the scaffold. She fixes his clothing, folds his hands across his chest. She sits and looks out
towards the woods.)*

PEARL. Who can say for certain what is witnessed the morning the minister bares his breast to Boston?

(Spot up on HIBBINS.)

HIBBINS. He rips off his shirt and right there on his chest's the letter *A,* like a brand, burned through all the way to the bone. That's when he kisses the girl and says she's his daughter. I always knew it. My master told me straight away.

(Spot up on BELLINGHAM.)

BELLINGHAM. He was valiant to the end, defending the right of the Prynne woman to keep her child no matter what. I believe the child was about to fall off the scaffold when he climbed up to save her. Must have been too much for his heart. Boston will miss him. He can never be replaced.

(Spot up on BRACKETT.)

BRACKETT. He gave his Election Day sermon and it was the most beautiful thing I have ever heard. I can't tell you what happened up there on the scaffold. I mean, with the storm and the bell that wouldn't stop chiming, it was difficult to tell. He took his shirt off, through. And I think he might have been bleeding and meant to use the shirt as a tourniquet. He was very hungry that morning. That much I know.

(Spots down on BELLINGHAM, BRACKETT and HIBBINS. Lights up on CHILLINGWORTH at the prison door. He

*very carefully picks all the blooms off the rose bush and
places them in his black bag.)*

PEARL. The minister's funeral is a simple affair Governor
Bellingham manages to speak badly at great length. At the
graveyard, only Master Brackett witnesses the minister's remains laid to rest. The Governor lives long enough to see his
sister hanged as a witch. And Master Brackett, having nothing better to do, drinks himself to death. Chillingworth remains indoors, and mostly, Boston forgets he's there. Within
the year, he dies. His body is discovered at the prison door, his
hand reaching out for what we do not know. Before he dies he
manages to write a will. And so, I am an heiress.

*(CHILLINGWORTH snaps his bag shut. He exits through the
prison doorway.)*

PEARL. I develop a fondness for water and sail away from
Boston forever. I keep watch for solid ground, but can't seem
to find it. And what of Hester? For a time she leaves Boston
and no one strays too close to her cottage, that cottage with so
many windows overlooking the sea. But one day, when Boston least expects it, Hester returns to her cottage and reclaims
the scarlet letter. Many seek her advice, and she is patient and
kind to them all. When finally she dies, Boston cannot recall
why it was she wore the scarlet letter in the first place. She is
buried in what by now is the old graveyard, where there is yet
a single space in which to be laid, next to a man called
Dimmesdale, who nobody remembers, and for whom nobody
cares to mourn.

(The light has become very bright through PEARL'S speech. DIMMESDALE slowly sits up and reaches out to HESTER. HESTER turns to him, but they do not touch, the space between them a gulf that can never really be bridged.)

DIMMESDALE. Hester. Are we there yet?

BLACKOUT

END OF PLAY